God / Family / Country

A Soldier's Story Through His Poems

Written by
Claude Battey Sti.

Compiled by
Ken Mashburn

Daniel Gomez Enterprises, LLC

God / Family / Country

Written by Claude Battey Stillwell
Compiled by Ken Mashburn

Published by Daniel Gomez Enterprises LLC / August 2021
All Rights Reserved.

Printed in the United States of America

Foreword

God, Family, Country.

There are many books written about the WWII era, but none will touch your heart more than "God, Family, Country" poems by C.B. Stillwell. These poems will surely relate in remarkable detail his faith, love of his family, and pride in serving his country.

This book is to honor "The Greatest Generation" on the 75th anniversary of the end of WWII.

I want you to read our story! These are the memoirs and chronicles of a soldier, a man of faith, and his family. He was someone who was proud to serve his country and to protect its citizens.

These poems were written 75 years ago. Twelve years ago, my brother-in-law, Curt Morris, gathered all the poems from my aunt and put together a book for all the Stillwell family to enjoy. Throughout the years I would always glance at the poems, but never really sat down to read them. At the end of 2018, I was going through a difficult time. Then in January of 2019, my dad passed away. After his death, and a lot of self-reflection, I seemed to have a lot of time on my hands. During this period, I read these poems extensively. I would sit there reading them with tears running down my face. I realized one night that these poems were not written just for our family. They were also written for us to share with all the men and women who have served, and continue to serve, their country so proudly and courageously.

I asked my mom if she realized what we had here, the answer was a resounding yes! From that point, we decided it was time for our family to share these poems with the rest of the country. There is a common theme throughout the book, a subject that was very important to C.B.: family, faith, love of the city he grew up in, and proudly serving his country!

I hope people understand the sacrifices that the men and women in the armed services gave up so we can have the freedoms we share today. The anthem pays respect to the people who have risked their lives, been injured, or have died defending our country. Without these brave men and women, we would not have the privilege to live in the greatest country in the world. So please remember the contributions of these great patriots.

So, sit back and embrace a man's thoughts from a different era, a time when things were as simple as a typewriter and a thought. Back to a time when family, faith, and country were the foundation of humanity. These poems will make you laugh, cry, and touch your heart. Never forget the past for they are the roots of our future. Thank you from our family to yours!

Written By: Kenneth Mashburn

Acknowledgments

No book is the product of an individual effort. "God, Family and Country" is no exception. Special thanks to Suzy Copeland, Lewis Copeland, and Lynn Mashburn, without your input and help, this book would not have happened.

Thanks to the entire Stillwell family.

Claud Battey "CB" Stillwell November 27, 1917 – May 9, 2012
Wife: Lyndall Gillespie Stillwell June 28, 1921 – February 1, 2010

Daughter: Madeline Dunwoody May 24, 1938 – May 19, 2013
Husband: Jerry Dunwoody

   Moses Dunwoody May 11. 1961 – December 17, 2003
   Richard Dunwoody (Susan)
   Alison Dunwoody

Daughter: Suzanne Copeland
Husband: Lewis Copeland

   Keith Bryant (Lorie)
   Justin Bryant
   Faith Bryant
   Ashley Bryant

   Dana Czekalla (Martin)
   Jordan Czekalla
   Cameron Czekalla
   Elijah Czekalla
   Noah Czekalla

Brandon Bryant (Patti)
   Madison Bryant
   Zackery Bryant

Hannah Porter (Jordan)
Audrey Porter

Dawn Brown
Tyler Brown
Ramsey Brown

Daughter: Battey Lynn Mashburn
Husband: Bob Mashburn February 4, 1940 – January 24, 2019

Kenneth Mashburn
Jackson Mashburn
Charles Mashburn

Judy Morris (Curt)
Hailey Morris
Parker Morris

Special thanks to Curt Morris for putting the first book together so our family could enjoy these poems.

Thanks to Dawn Brown for helping me convert all of the poems to word documents. Without your help, it would have taken me months to retype all of the poems.

Thank you, Jack and Charlie, for helping your computer-challenged dad with all of the scanning and properly filing all of the documents accordingly. Your dad loves you very much!

Special thanks to Daniel Gomez for helping me re-find myself, for guidance on the front and back covers, and making this book become a reality.

Special thanks to the Rome Area History Center for providing the photos of downtown Rome, Georgia and the City Clock Tower.

A final special thanks to "The Greatest Generation" and all the men and women who sacrificed their lives in WWII so we can be blessed with the freedoms that we have today!

Introduction

Claude Battey "C.B." Stillwell, known as "Poppi" to his grandchildren, was born November 27, 1917, in Rome Georgia, to the late Oliver B. Stillwell and Mamie Lanham Stillwell. He married the love of his life, Lyndall Gillespie, on July 16, 1937, a marriage that prevailed for 72 years.

The Selective Service Board drafted him into the military on January 10, 1944. At that time, he had a wife and three young daughters, which showed the seriousness of World War II. He did his basic training at Scott Air force Base in St. Clair County, Illinois, and was an honor graduate of his class. He served his entire tour of duty with the U.S. Army 14th Emergency Rescue Boat Squadron that rescued downed pilots in the Pacific Theatre. When not actively rescuing pilots, he wrote many poems about his belief in God, his beloved family, the city of Rome, the country he loved, and the military life he experienced. He received his honorable discharge after almost two years of service on December 8, 1945.

C.B. was a long-time member of the Second Avenue Methodist Church where he served in multiple capacities including Choir Director, Sunday school teacher, and Lay-leader.

He was employed by the Rome Provision Company for over 72 years, reaching the position of General Manager, and even working part-time as a Sales Representative during his retirement well into his 80's.

One of the joys during his retirement was performing "shows" consisting of songs, jokes, and stories at the many assisted living homes in the Rome area. Even into his 90's, he continued to give back to his community.

We hope these poems will touch your heart and give insight into one man's journey as a World War II veteran. These poems have brought much pride and joy to our family over the years and have instilled a deep respect for those who honorably and faithfully served our country in very difficult times.

About These Poems

Poems are by CB Stillwell

Written between Easter and Christmas of 1945,
while in the US Army

Each chapter tells a story, not just in his poems, but in his life and what he stood for. I want everyone to truly appreciate what my Grandad did in writing these poems while in the Pacific Theatre during the middle of WWII.

Somehow, he managed to get a typewriter! To this day, we still cannot figure out how he managed to do this. To keep the uniqueness, originality, and personal touch of these poems, we have left one poem in each chapter in its original form. Keep in mind these poems were written 75 years. So sit back and enjoy!

Table of Contents

A Soldier's Prayer (Original)
A Soldier's Prayer
Chow Time Aboard Ship
Manila
Moon over Manilla
A Manilla Bar
Mosquitos of the Great Far East
That Men Might Fly Again
A Tribute to President Roosevelt
A G.I. Going Home
When I Go Home to Stay
Victory
But Not In Vain
Pull Up the Anchor
A Post War Plan

His Love Now Rules My Heart (Original)
His Love Now Rules My Heart
Make Me True
Jesus Wept Again Today
Peace Through Prayer
God's House is Everywhere

Should Death Catch Up With Me
Peace on Earth Again

May I See You Again (Original)
May I See You Again
You
Dearest Beloved
On the Lonely Side
My Heart Beats Just For You
A Picture of You
Linda
Easter Thoughts
Just Waiting
Sailing Back to You
I'm Returning To My Dreams
Letter From President Bush
Couple Celebrates 70 Years
Stillwell Still Bustling

Children (Original)
Children
My Little Girls
Our First Child
Brown Eyes
Curly Top
To Daddy - A Toast
No Other Like Mother
Dear Sis
The Pest
My Mother-In-Law #1
My Mother-In-Law #2

Thanks (Original)
Thanks
The Meaning of a Friend
It's Morning Again
Evening
The Morning After the Night Before
The Wonders of Nature
Spring
The Wind

I Left My Heart in New Orleans (Written for George Bulrice)
(Original)
I Left My Heart in New Orleans (Written For George Bulrice)
Do You Remember (Written for George Shelvin)
A Reminder of Love (Written For George Wieser)
Thoughts of You (Written For Lt. Chapman)

Home is Where the Heart Is (Original)
Home is Where the Heart Is
What is Rome
The Hills of Rome
The City Clock

Last Word: The Family Blessing (Isaiah 59:21)

THE WHITE HOUSE
WASHINGTON

TO MEMBERS OF THE UNITED STATES ARMY EXPEDITIONARY
FORCES:

You are a soldier of the United States Army.

You have embarked for distant places where
the war is being fought.

Upon the outcome depends the freedom of your
lives: the freedom of the lives of those you love—
your fellow-citizens—your people.

Never were the enemies of freedom more
tyrannical, more arrogant, more brutal.

Yours is a God-fearing, proud, courageous
people, which, throughout its history, has put its
freedom under God before all other purposes.

We who stay at home have our duties to
perform—duties owed in many parts to you. You will
be supported by the whole force and power of this
Nation. The victory you win will be a victory of all
the people—common to them all.

You bear with you the hope, the confidence,
the gratitude and the prayers of your family, your
fellow-citizens, and your President—

Franklin D Roosevelt

Chapter 1

The War

A SOLDIERS PRAYER

Oh Father, dear Saviour of all men,
Hear Thou my prayer.
Rid this world the evils of sin,
Make peace come everywhere.

Dear Lord be with our loved ones,
And all our friends at home.
Protect them with Thy presence,
While o'er this world I roam.

We pray for our oppressors,
The cause of all this strife,
That they will leave the darkness,
And find eternal life.

Remember our friends and buddies,
Whose life they so freely gave,
In battles here and yonder,
So freedom would be saved.

Oh God be with the loved ones
Of our men everywhere,
So when this war is over,
They can return without a care.

Father, Thou has heard my prayer,
So if it be thy will,
Answer it and stop this fight,
So troubled hearts might thrill.

A SOLDIER'S PRAYER

Oh, Father, dear Savior of all men, hear thou my prayer,
rid this world the evils of sin, make peace come everywhere.

Dear Lord be with our loved ones, and all our friends at home,
protect them with Thy presence, while o'er this world I roam.

We pray for our oppressors, the cause of all this strife,
that they will leave the darkness, and find eternal life.

Remember our friends and buddies, whose life they so freely gave,
in battles here and yonder, so freedom would be saved,

Oh God be with the loved ones of our men everywhere,
so when this war is over, they can return without a care.

Father, thou has heard my prayer, so if it be thy will,
answer it and stop this fight, so troubled hearts might thrill.

CHOW TIME ABOARD SHIP

When you hear a whistleblowing or the sound of running feet,
you can be sure it's chow time when all will go to eat.

Each section forms their lines up according to number or card,
to wait their turn to hit the deck, this part is awful hard.

Someone sounds off your number, up the stairs you start to go,
a few steps you take, and someone says, get back until I let you
know.

Finally, you get up topside, but you've still a long way to go,
from bow to stern then down the steps, to the galley far below.

You reach the door but can't go in before you stands a guard,
who makes quite sure it is your turn, and then he'll punch your
card.

You've succeeded in reaching the galley, and now fully ready to eat,
pick up a plate, cup, and fork, but find no knife to cut your meat.

Someone pushes you from behind, someone else hits you in the
side,
K.P.'s yelling on every hand, while you stumble, slip and slide.

You start down the serving line, at last, you've reached your goal,
but the way the food is put on your plate would make a preacher
lose his soul.

The first you get is a piece of meat, so small it can hardly be seen,
a spoonful of carrots or maybe peas, and potatoes with peelings
unclean.

Then you will get a piece of cake, or peaches and coffee too,
then try to find a place to stand as someone pushes you.

You finally get a place at the table, then settle down to eat,
then find the peaches are in the peas and coffee all over the meat.

The bread is hard, the butter old, the coffee awful thin,
you think of the meals there back at home and wonder when you'll
get them again.

The ship will rock, your place will slide, but finally, the food goes
down,
then once again you go topside and pray for some solid ground.

You'll wish that the voyage was over, and you'll soon know how to
feel,
 to sit down at the table at home and enjoy a good quiet meal.

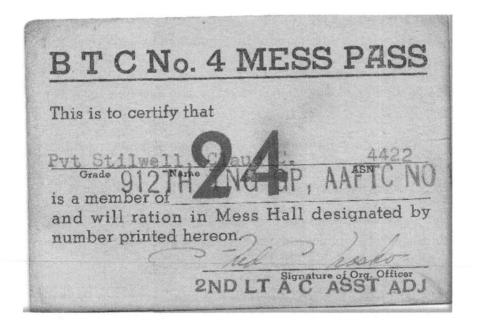

MANILA

This was once a beautiful city a few short years ago,
with it's churches so big and beautiful it's bridges with rivers below.

It's buildings so tall and stately, the streets so long and wide,
beaches that were always crowded and homes by the ocean side.

Close by there was a walled city, with it's convents and churches inside,
Where centuries past the world was told, that a saviour for us had died.

This city was the pearl of the orient, the pride of the great far east,
It's people free and happy, always joyful and full of peace.

The city is now in wreckage, it's streets no longer gay,
The buildings and churches are torn down and it's bridges washed away.

This was caused by the evil and treachery from the land of the rising sun,
It's soldiers came in to wreck it's peace, with bayonet, shell and gun.

For three years they held the city, destroying and causing pain,
Keeping prisoners in dungeons deep, never to see again.

Then came the forces of deliverance led by a man well known,
To help its people win the fight, which before they had fought alone.

The battle for the city soon was over on both sides many men died,
Its ports were filled with sunken ships, pushed about by the ocean's tide.

Our forces had won the battle, men died but not in vein,
The enemy was pushed into the hills, the people were free again.

Now some light are burning some cars you see pass by,
The people too now walk about, though not without a sigh.

Sometime in the future years, all the lights will shine again,
The people then can forget their tears, their strife, fears and pain.

The churches to will open up, their steeples near the sky,
That people can worship again as they please the Father that's still
on high.

MOON OVER MANILA

Moon over Manila, so lovely there in the sky,
moon over Manila, sending light from there on high.

Your beams reaching out to lovers, throughout this world below,
Filling their hearts with joy devin, making lips say, I love you so.

Moon over Manila, filling a tropic night,
With shadows soft and beautiful, with scenes of pure delight.

Moon over Manila, shining for you and me,
Moon over manila, making love so pure and free,

Floating through space up there above, passing each twinkling star,
Seeming to say, "I Love You Dear", no matter where you are.

Moon over Manila, please don't go away,
From the skies above, send down your love, so lovers will always be
gay.

A MANILA BAR

While walking down the avenue, no matter where you are,
in Manila, one can always find a rum or whiskey bar.

The signs outside will welcome you, the girls say come on in,
for this is the place to have some fun, and you can always meet a
friend.

Inside the smoke is terrible, you can hardly see the band,
making music with a horn or two, and a piano on a stand.

Sometimes you hear a solo, in a voice usually off-key,
but there's no need to grumble, for this is always free.

You decide to have a drink or two, take a table on the side,
order a shot of jungle juice, something you haven't tried.

It's brought to you by a pretty girl, who says two pesos please,
you hardly notice the shot she brought, for trying to see her knees.

The drink wouldn't fill a thimble, just enough for one small nip,
nothing like the good old days, when you carried it on your hip.

It's hard to stop with a drink or two because you get that feeling,
so let's have some fun and shoot the works, and the girls look so
appealing.

The bank will play hot music, the kind you like so much,
the girls will smile, flirt, and sing, but their custom is do no touch.

Soon an M.P. comes strolling by, says pal it's time to go,
get off the street by 11 pm thought maybe you didn't know.

The last drink does down, and you start to leave the table,
it's probably good you had to leave, cause soon you wouldn't be
able.

This is the end of a glorious night, no dancing, no girls, but not bad, there's plenty of fun in a Manila bar if you forget and just feel glad.

When you return to the USA, to get all the stuff you've been missing,
good whiskey, a bar, a first-class band, and girls that don't mind kissing.

Just don't forget the good old days, in Manilla where life was gay, but of course, it's nothing at all to compare with the things in the USA.

MOSQUITOES OF THE GREAT FAR EAST

I've traveled this wide world over and studied all the birds and beasts,
but here I've found the worst of all, the mosquitoes of the great far east.

They will bite you every morning, chase you every night,
follow you where you go, and sting with all their might.

At night when you are sleeping and dreaming of Hody Lamar,
they buzz your head like a P38 no matter where you are.

You can battle them with a swatter, spray them with a gun,
and a minute later they're back again, ready to make a run.

I've cussed them during work time. I've cussed them while at play,
but nothing yet I've said or done, would run those insects away.

There's one type that makes us worry, no matter if we're married or single,
that is the kind we find on us sitting at a forty-five-degree angle.

For this is the kind the doctors say is the worst of these son-of-a-bitches,
for they will give you the kind of germ that does much more than itches.

These damn mosquitoes are terrible. They are always after your blood,
they will suck you dry at every chance, even if you are lying in the mud.

It seems to be a funny thing, how they work long after dark,
we can pull the cover-up to our ears, but still, they hit the mark.

There's a story of how one landed on an airstrip one evening later, his belly was filled with gasoline, they thought it was a P38.

When you're sitting in the moonlight, gazing into a pretty face, the mosquitoes drop down from up above, and sting as you embrace.

Each day we take our Atabrine, to keep us healthy, they say, but I don't think it would be necessary if these mosquitoes would go away.

We have won the war with Germany, with Japan we cannot fail, still there's a battle we'll never win, the mosquitoes with the stinging tail.

If you don't believe this story, then I will prove it to you, just take a trip to the great far east, then soon you'll find it's true.

THAT MEN MIGHT FLY AGAIN

On every sea and ocean wide, in storms or pouring rain,
you will find the crash boats on the job, that men might fly again.

These boats are small and speedy, strong enough to stand the strain,
of going out on stormy seas, to rid some man of pain.

At times their guns are blazing, at enemies in the sky,
and even though their score is low, the crash boats always try.

You will find them near the beaches, where a battle is being won,
so just in case a plane might fall, they can save some mother's son.

Sometimes their task is not confined, to the job of saving men,
but that of carrying needed supplies, that some might fly again.

Their crews are small, their quarters tight, sometimes they work in rain,
or beneath the heat of a blazing sun, but these men do not complain.

You'll see these boats soon speeding when they hear an SOS,
the urgent call of a crashing plane, or a ship that's in distress.

The crash boats don't want any glory, the crews no battle praise,
they only want to do their job, until the voice of victory can raise.

So until the fight is over, and we all go home to rest,
you will find the crash boats on the job, waiting for a call of distress.

When we have won the victory, and return to our loved one's side,
we'll tell them stories of greatness, of men that might have died.

When the story of this war is written, some pages will surely explain,
the part played by the crash boats, that men might fly again.

A TRIBUTE TO PRESIDENT ROOSEVELT

The other day, God called away to His mansions up above,
a man so great and loyal, so true and full of love.

His task on earth was not complete, there was much he'd planned to do,
to make this mighty world of ours, peaceful, kind, and true.

But God has called him to his home, he did for the world his part,
had strived to make this land of ours, better from the start.

He held many high positions in our country, the greatest of all,
when he climbed to be our leader, never to let us fall.

He led us through great depressions, we found him to be our guide,
and followed him in every way, until for our land he died.

He spoke to all his people in a voice so strong and clear,
in a language all could understand, he taught us not to fear.

He spoke with thoughts of kindness, our troubles would always share,
the whole world listened to his fireside chats, some which ended with a prayer.

He inspired the people of all nations, no matter what color or creed,
because he was willing to lend a hand and help all in time of need.

Though sick in body and restless, sometimes bent with pain,
he gave his all to the very end, for our world he stood the strain.

For all he had a kindly word, to everyone he gave a smile,
when tired, would visit his Georgia home, where he could rest awhile.

A G.I. GOING HOME

I was called out this morning and told to look alive,
report to headquarters, the sergeant said, as your points are eighty-
five.

I struggled into my uniform, didn't bother to lace a shoe,
ran down to see the company C.O., to see if this was true.

I rushed right in, gave a salute, said, "Sir, did you call for me,
the sergeant just said I had enough points so that you could set me
free."

The Lt. said, "You can be at ease, said Jones you can get out,
just sign your name on the dotted lines, and we'll see what this is
about."

I signed the papers here and there, army red tape is so much
trouble,
but the wonderful news of going home, had me signing my name on
the double.

He said, "Turn in your field gear, your carbine and canteen too,
have all your clothes and equipment here, or it won't be good for
you."

So I opened up my barracks bag, started checking the stuff I had,
found I was short most everything, for me it did look bad.

I remembered swapping one pants and shirt, to a flip for a bottle of
booze,
a pair of shoes, a blanket or two, all the things I didn't use.

I thought these things were expendable, for free we could get
plenty more,
but when I saw that statement of charges, I darn near hit the floor.

The CO said he would call me back, if and when my release went through,
the proper channels it would have to go before he would know what to do.

Three long weeks I waited, looking for the papers to come back,
but not a word did I hear, gosh was I a sad sack.

Then at last I was rewarded, it was official I was going home,
would leave at once on a troopship, and soon be free to roam.

I was getting out of the army, leaving all that chicken behind,
at last going back to the state I love, where friends and family I would find.

Now this doesn't end my story, there's so much I could tell,
the things I'll do when I hit the states, I'm really gonna raise some hell.

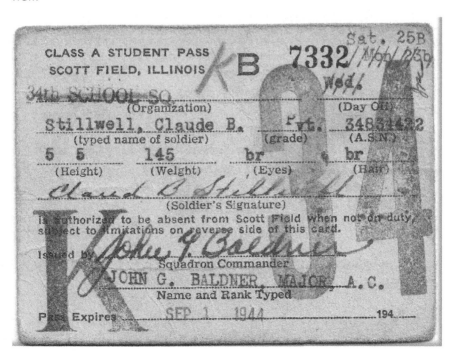

WHEN I GO HOME TO STAY

Since the minute I entered the service, since the morning I went away,
I've thought about the things I'll do when I go home to stay.

What a wonderful day it will be, when I board that ship that sails,
over the wide Pacific, to the Golden Gate, then for home I'll take the rails.

When the train pulls into the station, at home where I long to be,
I'll look out and see the ones I love, and know at least I'm free.

This war has caused heartaches, things have changed since I went away,
but sadness will turn to gladness when I go home to stay.

I will try to be a good father, tomorrow, same as yesterday,
with the same kind of love, they knew before when I go home to stay.

I will feel so good to walk down the street, my family by my side,
doing the things we used to do with our hearts filled with pride

So listen, start getting things ready, be prepared for a happy day,
our happiness will start all over again when I go home to stay.

VICTORY

Listen to the whistles blowing, watch the flares shooting through the sky,
hear the noise everyone is making, see old glory waving there on time.

See the smiles on all the happy faces, see the tears of joy in their eyes,
hear the laughter of the soldiers and sailors, or the prayers of mothers and wives.

Hear the church bells ringing from the steeples, telling us that victory now is here,
giving out a message filled with gladness, telling us to banish all our fear.

See the band as it marches on parade, its songs of victory filling the air,
out in front, our flag is proudly waving, a peace we all can share.

Our people are celebrating a victory, throughout the world, the battles now have ceased,
now may God grant us freedom forever, and the joys of lasting peace.

BUT NOT IN VAIN

The victory has been won over our aggressors, battles have ceased, through this might earth,
yet for years we'll see the pain and all the heartaches we'll see the misery and strife the war gave birth.

We'll see a father as he walks down the avenue, with a heavy heart, though proud of some battle won,
he has given much to win our countries freedom, for, in this battle, he gave an only son.

There goes a sailor, look he is on crutches, still, he's thinking not of selfish strife,
though thankful that God above took pity, he gave a leg but saved another life.

We hear a mother talking very softly, telling of her youngest son who dies,
he led the way to attack an enemy outpost, was first to die, because he was the guide.

Here young man, may I help you across the street, so healthy looking yet plain he cannot see,
he gave his eyes when a shell exploded near him, lost his sight, to make our country free.

We see a child whose daddy did not return, she remembers his kiss, his last time to say goodbye,
perhaps behind those sad eyes she's thinking, why, oh why, did daddy have to die?

There's a wife, she's reading some old letters, it's all that's left of the one she loved so dear,
one says, my darling, please do not worry, in life or death, we'll always be near.

Through the years we'll still see signs of battle, time alone can heal the scars and pain,
through anguish, grief, and death we won the victory, kept our freedom, which forever will remain.

General Joseph W. Stilwell (facing camera) Tenth Army commander on Okinawa chats with an unidentified Chinese general at the Jap surrender signing aboard the U.S.S. Missouri.

PULL UP THE ANCHOR

Pull up the anchor, we're sailing home across the great blue sea,
we're going back to those we love, where life is sweet and free.

Pull up the anchor, get underway, give the signal full steam ahead,
before many days I hope to sleep in my own soft snowy bed.

Let's cross the ocean wide and blue, make the trip in record time,
let's get to the states in time to hear, the bells of Thanksgiving
chime.

Pull up the anchor, we're all aboard, returning from battles won,
we fought a good fight, won the war, now it's time to have some
fun.

We don't mind the crowded conditions, where we sleep down in
the hole,
or the beans we get for breakfast, on top of our coffee roll.

We can stand our stomach tossing, be too sick to even die,
the heat below, the wind above, take it all without a sigh.

Because we're taking that homeward journey, going back where we
belong,
through the golden gate, to the ones that wait, in prayer, gladness,
and song.

A POST WAR PLAN

We all dream of the future, the things we plan to do,
when again we reach that land of ours, after the war is through.

Some plan to go into business, others to jobs at home,
then there's some to be satisfied, must continue this world to roam.

Some will marry their sweethearts, the ones who waited back there,
and start a home of happiness, with love and dreams to share.

But I don't have one postwar plan, I have a thousand rolled into one,
It's not a wife, or to build a home, and it's not just to have some fun.

Because you see, I've had those things, for many years passed by,
a loving wife, a home and kids, a job with salary high.

So my postwar plan will be complete, when I get that last release,
a discharge paper, my ticket home, returning to a life of peace.

For I know when I get back home, I'll find things as before,
my home, my kids, a loving wife, and peace forevermore.

Perhaps we'll find new happiness, our home we might expand,
but my return safely to the ones' I love, is my greatest post war plan.

He strived to lead this world of ours to a goal of lasting peace,
and for this cause, he lived and died, but his efforts will never cease.

Though God has called him up above to his home where there is no pain,
his unselfish efforts while here on earth, in the people, will always remain.

This world of ours will never forget his courage, his smiling face,
his friendly voice as he said "My friends", these things we cannot replace.

Like a soldier in battle he gave his life for his country though not in vain,
he died for the cause of freedom, a freedom which will always remain.

G R A D U A T I O N

Second Area Theater   24 October 1944
                              1645
                    Scott Field, Illinois

INVOCATION   Chaplain Lee P. Ward

ADDRESS AND PRESENTATION
   OF DIPLOMAS   Major John D. Gantz

ARMY AIRWAYS COMMUNICATIONS SYSTEM
   Classes 56, 9, 46, 2, 10

HONOR GRADUATES

Pvt. Harry M. Grace   Pvt. Herschel G. Hammack
Pvt. Chester C. Cox   Pvt. Albert J. Appleby, Jr.
Pvt. Claud B. Stillwell   Pvt. Ljudimir M. Yama
                    Pvt. John F. Fullen

RADIO OPERATOR AND MECHANICS COURSE
   Class 97

HONOR GRADUATE

                    Pvt. Mendel T. Gordon

MEDLEY   'The Stylists'
(Marian Beckman - Soloist)

B E N E D I C T I O N

NATIONAL ANTHEM

COL. THOMAS W. HASTEY   COMMANDING OFFICER
COL. N. L. COTE   DEPUTY FOR TRAINING AND
                                             OPERATIONS
MAJ. GORDON A. DOUGLAS   DIRECTOR OF TECHNICAL
                                             TRAINING
MAJ. RICHARD E. HEYL   DIRECTOR OF MILITARY
                                             TRAINING

ENLISTED MAN'S TEMPORARY PASS

Stillwell Claude E.   Pfc.   34834422

      (Name)   (Grade)   (Army serial No.)

Atchd. Unssgd. Sep. C. Ft. McPherson, Ga.

      (Organization)   (Station)

is authorized to be absent—

From 1800 6 Dec. 1945   To 0730 7 Dec. 1945

To visit   Atlanta, Ga.

Signed *George R Kimberly Jr. 1st Lt*

                           Commanding Officer, CAC

*W. D., A. G. O. Form No. 7   (OVER)

     26 June 1943

* This form supersedes W. D., A. G. O. Form No. 7, 8 September 1942, which may be used until existing stocks are exhausted.

Chapter 2

A Man's Faith

HIS LOVE NOW RULES MY HEART

Yes His love now rules my heart so completely,
since the day I opened it and let Him in,
Jesus can rid your heart of all its' worry,
Its' evil thoughts, its fears, the presence of all sin.

Yes His love now rules my heart so completely,
His love will carry me through all my strife,
since I opened up my heart and let him enter,
I'm free of sin, and have eternal life.

Yes my soul was black, my heart was filled with evil,
until His shining face, looked down at me,
then all the clouds of darkness started disappearing,
His light I know, will shine through all eternity.

Giving joy to those whose heart is filled with sadness,
Giving strength and love to those weak in soul,
Giving all the world His life for their salvation,
helping all to reach a heavenly goal.

Yes His love now rules my heart so completely,
and I know that he alone will be my guide,
since I opened up my heart and let Him enter,
I know that He is always by my side.

To music of Ah Sweet Mystery of Life.

HIS LOVE NOW RULES MY HEART

Yes, His love now rules my heart so completely, since the day I opened it and let him in,
Jesus can rid your heart of all its worry, its evil thoughts, its fears, the presence of all sin.
Yes, His love now rules my heart so completely, His love will carry me through all my strife,
since I opened up my heart and let him enter, I'm free of sin, and have eternal life.
Yes, my soul was black, my heart was filled with evil until His shining face looked down at me,
then all the clouds of darkness started disappearing, His light I know will shine through all eternity.
Giving joy to those whose heart is filled with sadness, giving strength and love to those weak in soul,
giving all the world His life for their salvation, helping all to reach a heavenly goal.
Yes, His love now rules my heart so completely, and I know that he alone will be my guide,
since I opened up my heart and let Him enter, I know that He is always by my side.

To the music of Ah Sweet Mystery of Life.

MAKE ME TRUE

Dear Lord let me be a friend to men, Father make me true,
give me a heart that's free of sin, and one that's kindly too.

Instill in me a heart that's pure, a mind with naught to hide,
let me repent, then make me sure that you'll be by my side.

Dear God give to me a life that's worthy of thy love,
though I feel much pain and strife, keep my eyes looking above.

Fill my soul with prayerful thoughts, my body with strength to give,
a helping hand to those who brought, such strife here where I live.

Father give to me a voice to speak, one that is full of song,
let me lead others whose souls Thy seek to teach me to do no
wrong.

Make me, Father, willing to share to any who may be in need,
give me time to kneel in prayer, forgive me of sin, I plead.

Forgive me Father, the bad I've done, with Thy power cleanse my
soul,
and then God, if thy favor I've won, after this life give me a
heavenly goal.

This prayer Father, I've sent to thee, for thy sill I wish to do,
thou saved others, so please save me, then Lord, make me true.

JESUS WEPT AGAIN TODAY

Jesus wept again today, as He looked from heaven above,
and saw what was happening to the children of the Father He
dearly loves.

Jesus wept again today, as He saw the flags unfurled,
and knows what's within the blacked hearts, of the men trying to
rule the world.

Jesus wept again today, though not on Calvary,
he wept because he must have failed when he died for you and me.

Jesus wept again today, looking down on oceans wide,
as he prayed for the soul of every man, in this watery grave has
died.

Jesus wept again today, as he saw the bleeding heart,
of a silver-haired mother down below, whose son died at the start.

Jesus wept again today, when He saw a young man die,
he heard the sobs of His loved ones, as he went to His home in the
sky.

Jesus wept again today, looking down on desert sands,
he felt the pain of the dying, as He stood with outstretched hands.

Jesus wept again today, looking down from his home on high,
as he saw the brave men dying in a fight to control the sky.

Jesus wept again today, his eyes on jungles wide,
he heard the prayers of the dying, is always by their side.

Jesus wept again today, when He heard a young child cry,
she knew her father, who had gone away, had returned to his place
in the sky.

Jesus wept again today, his eyes on a mother who received,
a message that tells of one and only son who died for the cause he
believed.

Jesus wept again today, His heart was filled with pain,
his eyes on every cross below, which tells of loved ones slain.

Jesus wept again today, for a world so full of strife,
he hears each groan, he feels each pain, as each shell destroys a
life.

Jesus wept again today, at the things within his sight,
his sweat again turned to blood, as He prayed to make men right.

Jesus wept again today, His world is torn apart,
he sees the ruins of countless things, which left an empty heart.

PEACE THROUGH PRAYER

People at home are working, striving every day,
building all the things of war, but some forgot to pray.

Some have the wrong impression, They think war is a game,
where one side wins the victory, the other goes down in shame.

They know we soldiers are fighting on battlefields everywhere,
they will send us guns and equipment, but never think of prayer.

Some will say when the day is done, and they come home to rest,
I worked eight hours, I did my share; but does God think it's their
best?

You'll find some in the night clubs, being gay with drink and song,
they too will say, we did our part, but God knows they are wrong.

We will continue winning victories, because God is on our side,
but we will never win the peace, until we let Him be our guide.

There is only one way of bringing peace, and it's not by men or
might,
but by all people falling on their knees asking God to end the fight.

God knows all our worries, our grief he'll always share,
if only we will lift our eyes, and go to Him in prayer.

Ask Him to be our guiding light, on the ground and in the air,
if it be his will to stop the fight, and He'll give us peace through
prayer.

So no matter how hard you're working, or what you are willing to
share,
remember that your job's not done, until you go to God in prayer.

If we are to win the fight, and return to our homes back there, everyone must do what's right, and ask God for peace through prayer.

GOD'S HOUSE IS EVERYWHERE

We find God's house most everywhere, in towns and villages small,
or cities big and beautiful near buildings wide and tall.

We find God's house in the countryside near a winding road or
stream,
where people worship as they please in a cabin neat and clean.

We find God's house in the valleys or among the sloping hills,
where the word of God is brought to all that troubled hearts might
thrill.

We find God's house in chapels large, in building old or small,
all teaching from the Holy Book which saves men one and all.

We find God's house on the avenues or the end of a dirty street,
where the people meet in song and prayer to make their lives
complete.

We find God's house on the battlefields where our chaplains strong
and brave,
pour out their hearts to dying men whose soul they seek to save.

We find God's house in the jungles in a clearing beneath the sky,
where men might give their hearts to God before they go out to die.

We find God's house in the desert in the heat and rolling sand,
where men can meet and ask their God to lend a helping hand.

We find God's house in the trenches or behind some prison wall,
we find that God is everywhere to answer our every call.

We find God's house in the submarines on the largest ships at sea,
the word of God goes far and wide that all men might be free.

We find God's house in the skies above in the planes that fly up there,
for the pilots know within their hearts that God will always care.

So you see, God's house is everywhere, in the air, on land, and on the sea,
so people can worship Almighty God through all eternity.

Second Avenue United Methodist Church   Rome, Georgia

SHOULD DEATH CATCH UP WITH ME

Should death catch up with me somewhere along the way?
I'll leave this earth with not a fear when God takes me away.

Should death catch up with me before my duties here are done?
It won't be bad to leave this earth for heaven with freedom won.

Should death catch up with me, should a bullet still my heart,
it won't be that I've died in vain, but to give freedom another start.

Should death catch up with me, I'll leave my loved ones here,
the ones that made my life worthwhile, and taught me not to fear.

Should death catch up with me, if God calls me above,
I know that in some future day, I'll again see those I love.

Should death catch up with me, let's have no tears or sadness,
for I'm going to a better place, where there's nothing but joy and
gladness.

Should death catch up with me from God I've naught to hide,
while on this earth, I tried to be, always by his side.

Should death catch up with me, God's smiling face I'll see,
I'll live above with the heavenly hosts through all eternity.

PEACE ON EARTH AGAIN

Long years ago a Savior was born, God gives to free a world of sin,
he sent to a world, weak and forlorn, to bring peace and goodwill to
men.

He died on the cross to make His job complete, before returning to
His Father above,
with wounds in His side, nails through His feet, His life He gave up
for love.

Long years have passed since that glorious day, the world again
filled with sin and greed,
people forgot and turned away, from the Christ, who had tried to
lead.

Nations strived for power, forgot about peace, went onto battle
with flags unfurled,
the good against evil, trying to cease, the horrors of a sin-torn
world.

The forces of evil were winning the fight until our Savior took a
hand,
He gathered our forces, showed us the light, gave us strength to
save our land.

The fighting was hard, the road was long, to the end where victory
lay,
we fought with courage, prayer, and song, to drive the oppressors
away.

After years of hardships and untold strife, filled with death, blood,
and pain,
we won the fight, saved freedoms life brought peace on earth
again.

Now we have won the victory here on earth, men died but not in
vain,
for they helped give freedom another birth and brought peace on
earth again.

Chapter 3

Family (Lyndall)

MAY I SEE YOU AGAIN

I remember so well the first night we met
all the crazy things I said,
Explaining in detail the places I had been,
and the books that I had read.

It seems that you were dating another boy,
I saw you as I stopped in the street,
Something was wrong with your boyfriends' car,
so this is how we chanced to meet.

That winters night was dark and cold,
no signs of snow or rain,
But oh how my heart was knocking,
when I asked, may I see you again.

We rode out through the countryside,
sometimes you would guide the car,
But since your folks were out of town
we couldn't go very far.

You said,"I must be home by ten o'clock
or grandmother will tan my hide,
But please come back some other time,
and again we'll go to ride."

So back we started to your house
even though iI did complain,
And kissed you for the very first time,
then said,"May I see you again?"

As our lips met in heavenly bliss,
the world went round and round,
I knew at once you were meant for me,
a mate at last I had found.

We talked about most everything,
though I hardly know what we said,
You tried to be such a lady then forgot,
and said, wonder if grandma has gone to bed.

So this is how it started,
a love which will always remain,
Agoodnight kiss at ten o'clock,
then I asked," may I see you again?"

con't

May I See You Again   con't

It's been eight years since our first night,
but still it's very plain,
If I see you a million more times,
I'll say," May I see you again?"

To Lyndall

MAY I SEE YOU AGAIN

I remember so well the first night we met, all the crazy things I said,
explaining in detail the places I had been, and the books that I had
read.

It seems that you were dating another boy, I saw you as I stopped in
the street,
something was wrong with your boyfriend's car, so this is how we
chanced to meet.

That winter's night was dark and cold, no signs of snow or rain,
but oh how my heart was knocking, when I asked, "May I see you
again?"

We rode out through the countryside, sometimes you would guide
the car,
but since your folks were out of town, we couldn't go very far.

You said, "I must be home by ten o'clock or grandmother will tan
my hide,
but please come back some other time, and again we'll go to ride."

So back we started to your house even though I did complain,
and kissed you for the very first time, then said, "May I see you
again?"

As our lips met in heavenly bliss, the world went round and round,
I knew at once you were meant for me, a mate, at last, I had found.

We talked about almost everything, though I hardly know what we
said,
you tried to be such a lady then forgot, and said, wonder if grandma
has gone to bed.

So this is how it started, a love that will always remain,
a goodnight kiss at ten o'clock, then I asked, "May I see you again?"

42

It's been eight years since our first night, but still, it's very plain,
If I see you a million more times, I'll say, "May I see you again?"

To: Lyndall

YOU

Who did I meet some years ago on a cold winter's night,
while the moon was shining up above, throwing beams on lovely
light?

Who, while riding down the road with me, would sit far on her side,
and look at me with laughing eyes, as we enjoyed the ride.

And who was it I learned to love, right from the very start,
and knew that someday she'd be mine, never to go apart.

Who was it that stole my heart, at sixteen or before,
and sometimes by her actions, would make me awful sore?

And then in just a few short months, who said, "I'll be your wife,
will have your kids and cook for you, and love you all my life."

Then when we met the preacher, who said, "Of course I do,
I'll love, honor, and cherish, be always true to you."

And just a short while later, as we sat under a golden moon,
who whispered softly in my ear, a baby is coming soon.

Who during months of waiting, always had for me a smile,
even though her every muscle, was aching all the while.

Then the day soon rolled around, one we would remember long,
who said to me, "Don't worry dear, nothing will go wrong."

And who made a wonderful mother, for this child and others too,
even though the job was very hard, who said, "I'll see it through."

And as the years went passing by, who was always by my side,
who gave to me her very all, and proved to be my guide.

Who is it that's true to me, though we are miles apart,
and writes to me most every night, who loves me with all her heart?

And who is back there waiting, for that glad and happy day,
when we will be together again, forever there to stay.

Who each night do I pray for, asking God to keep her right,
to help her with each problem, and be her guiding light.

Who is it I'll always love, no matter where I roam,
who will I think of every day until I get back home?

Who will always be beautiful, even when old and gray,
and continue to have a winning charm, just as she has today.

Those eyes will keep on smiling, through the joys or sorrows we share,
who will be my shining light, about who will I always care.

Who will I cherish always, same as from the very start,
whose love will I always try to hold, until death do us part?

To: Lyndall

DEAREST BELOVED

Dearest beloved,

Tonight I'm thinking of years gone by, the ones you've made so happy for me,
the times we spent with hardly a sign, just as it ought to be.

I'm thinking too how lucky I've been, to have married a girl like you,
with charm, beauty, a heart free of sin, one who will always be true.

You have filled the clouds with sunshine, made nights turn into day,
since you promised always to be mine, to go with me all the way.

Dearest beloved, my memories of you are clear, even though the haze of battle strife,
for in my heart you're always near, and will be all my life.

It's thoughts of you that make me strong when dangers come my way,
I know to you I'll always belong, no matter what others say.

You filled my heart with happiness by staying by my side,
made my life one of heavenly bliss, you have filled my soul with pride.

Dearest beloved, you've been so kind and fair, made life for me such a wonderful thrill,
I've had your love to share, and pray to God I always will.

For me the sun will always shine, the skies will always be blue,
as long as your heart is close to mine, and I can be with you.

Dearest beloved, it's time that we must part, for I have here a job to do,
so remember dear with all my heart, I'll keep on loving you.

To: Lyndall

ON THE LONELY SIDE

Knowing dear that you are so far away, and we can't meet for many a day,
the memories of you I cannot hide, because I'm on the lonely side.

Your smile, your laughter was always gay, a kind word to all whether at work or play,
your gentle way, your winning charm, the way you talked and held my arm.

The way you laughed, sand, and walked, your smiling eyes, the way you talked,
those secret things you would confide, it's true, I'm on the lonely side.

Sweetheart no one could ever replace, the way you loved, your kindly face.
the way you forgave when I did you wrong and said to you, I would always belong.

Remembering this about you there, each night I include this in my prayer,
that God will protect and guide you through, and send me back to be with you.

I've missed you dear since going away, my love for you grows more each day.
So dearest until together, we can abide, I'll continue to be on the lonely side.

To: Lyndall

MY HEART BEATS JUST FOR YOU

My heart beats just for you, dear, as it ticks out every day,
my heart beats only for you, whether near or far away.

It pumps a message to my brain, each second of each hour,
It says I'll always love you, dear, for me my only flower.

Without you here my dearest, life wouldn't mean a thing,
there wouldn't be any flowers, no birds to sing in the spring.

The sun above would cease to shine, the moon would go away,
with you darling, a life divine, without you, no night or day.

My heart beats just for you dear, it sends through me a cheer,
I'm full of pride, with you by my side, so dearest be always near.

To: Lyndall

A PICTURE OF YOU

Your picture means much to me, dear, while I'm so far away,
to see your face so lovely through every tiresome day.

The times I'm sad and lonely and wishing I were there with you,
I look at your picture there on the wall and know you're lonely too.

Your picture means much to me, dear, to see your smiling face,
brings back memories of days gone by, memories we cannot
replace.

It brings back thoughts of many things, our moments of heavenly
bliss,
When I could hold you in my arms, or steal from you a kiss.

And every night when I go to bed, I lie there and look at you,
and somehow feel you are very near, wishing it could be true.

Your picture means much to me, dear, to gaze into your eyes,
looking so blue and devilish, more beautiful than all the skies.

They sparkle just like the sunshine in the blue sky up above,
so gay, bright, and cheerful, too. I'm glad we fell in love.

Your picture means much to me dear, just how much, words can't
say,
so thanks for it a million times, it will bring me joy each day.

I sit and look for hours, at your lips, your lovely hair,
that neck so soft and beautiful, the smile that's always there.

Your picture means much to me, dear, I'll keep it while we're apart.
now darling I have your picture, but you still have my heart.

To: Lyndall

LINDA

I've crossed the oceans wide, not much I haven't tried, but you're always by my side, Linda.
No matter what I do, no matter what I view, I always think of you, Linda.

You're in my arms at night, how wonderful it can be,
when I close my eyes and go to sleep, it's always you I see.

Oh Linda my dearest, to me you're everything,
my pinup, my dream girls, the flowers that bloom in spring.

Oh be mine always darling, may our love forever remain,
let me prove to you, my love is true, my lovely Linda.

To: Lyndall

EASTER THOUGHTS

My darling on this Easter Day, I send my love from far away,
to you my dear so good and true, my love will always follow you.

While I'm away we share the pain, and will until we meet again,
until my duty here is done, I'm sure for us, there can be no fun.

As I kneel in prayer this Easter Day, and look to God and try to pray.
I think of us so far apart, but know we are near within our heart.

O'er this whole wide world I may have to roam,
but someday dear I'll come marching home.

Then I'll be with you, and the others I love,
until my Maker calls me to my home above.

To: Lyndall

JUST WAITING

I'm waiting for the day to come, when my country again I'll see,
the hills, the streams, the cities there, the place I long to be.

I'm waiting to hear that, "All aboard," a discharge in my hand,
to see the beauty of the Golden Gate, and the sights of my native land.

I'm waiting to see the one I love, to hold her in my arms,
To see the smile upon her face, and again have all her charms.

I'm waiting to hear the laughter, of the kids I left back there,
to see their smiling faces, their lives again to share.

I'm waiting for that happy home, the one I left behind,
to again know the joys of living, to have some peace of mind.

SAILING BACK TO YOU

I'm sailing back to you my love, recrossing this ocean wide,
I'm giving thanks to Him above, that I'll again be by your side.

Months have passed since I left you there, but you've had my heart
each day,
you were in my thoughts, my every dream, since the moment I
went away.

I'm sailing back to you sweetheart, returning there to live,
to be with you till the end of time, to share what I have to give.

I've helped to win the battles here, but now I'm glad we're through,
the war is over, I have you dear, and soon will be back with you.

I'm sailing back to you dear love, to the heaven I'll find with you,
I'll forget these months of battle strife, and the hardships we've
been through.

Because I'll see your smiling eyes, kiss your lips of pure delight,
together we'll be under God's blue skies, or watching His moon by
night.

I'm sailing back to you my darling, counting days till I'll again hold
your charms,
dreaming of your kiss, that heavenly bliss, of holding you in my
arms.

We'll soon drop anchor, I'll board a train, get on t hat Dixie line,
and once by your side I'll always remain, forever, for you are mine.

To: Lyndall

I'M RETURNING TO MY DREAMS

For months I've wished and waited, been away for years it seems,
but at last my troubles are over, for I'm returning to my dreams.

Each day was lonely, nights were long, life was so empty for me,
with never the joy, thrills or songs, that together we used to see.

My only joy was in my dreams because my dreams were thoughts
of you,
the things that we have done before, or what we're going to do.

I'm happy now, my joys complete, I know my dreams are coming
true,
because I'm returning to my dreams, and sweetheart my dreams
are you.

To: Lyndall

THE WHITE HOUSE

WASHINGTON

July 23, 2007

Mr. and Mrs. C. B. Stillwell
521 Laporte Street, S.E.
Rome, Georgia 30161

Dear Mr. and Mrs. Stillwell:

Congratulations on your 70th wedding anniversary.

Building a lasting marriage is a wonderful accomplishment and a great
joy. Your years together are an inspiration, and Laura and I wish you
many more years of love and happiness.

Best wishes on this special occasion.

Sincerely,

George W. Bush

Couple celebrates 70 years

C.B. and Lyndol Stilwell were married 70 years ago today.

> 'I thought she was the most beautiful woman I met my entire life. She still is.'.
>
> C.B. Stilwell
> of his wife Lyndol

C.B. and Lyndall Stillwell have been married since their teens.

YEARS from 1A

He still occasionally finds time to take walks and still rides his bicycle. A former choir director at his church, he also takes piano lessons and periodically sings at local nursing homes.

Needlework has been one of Mrs. Stillwell's favorite hobbies, and she also likes to read and work crossword puzzles.

In 2000, the couple, their daughters and their sons-in-law took an Alaskan cruise together, an event the family remembers fondly.

Two of their daughters, Madeline Dunwoody and Suzy Copeland, live in Rome. Lynn Mashburn lives in Cumming.

Stillwell still bustling

Routines, work keep this Roman busy, busy, busy

By MARK WILDER
Staff Writer

Profile
C.B. Stillwell

Roman C.B. Stillwell believes in long-term commitments and staying busy.

Many 77-year-olds settle into a more relaxed lifestyle during retirement. But somebody forgot to tell Stillwell to slow down.

"No, I haven't slowed down yet," Stillwell said with a smile recently. "I'm still going full-steam. I'll probably slow down when they throw dirt on my face."

Stillwell, who will turn 78 on Nov. 27, "retired" from the Curtis Packing Company in 1984 after working there for about 54 years.

Eleven years later, he can still be found at the business on many days, "helping out."

"I just work there when they can find me," Stillwell joked. "I don't suppose I'll ever really retire.

"Being there as long as I had, they probably felt I could be of some help to them. If somebody's out, I take a route or fill in at the office, whatever they need," he said.

After returning from World War II service in December 1945, Stillwell returned to the company and began traveling the roads of north Georgia. He then became the plant manager, the position he held until 1984.

"I was on the road for a lot of years," he said. "I covered Atlanta starting after the war and worked that area for about 15 years."

About three years ago, Stillwell and his wife of 58 years, Lyndall, drove about 3,500 miles on the road during a vacation.

"We don't do that all that often, but we enjoyed that a lot," he said. "We went all over the country — New York, Niagara Falls and everywhere in between.

"It's good to get out and let your hair down every once in a while, if you've got any hair," Stillwell said, laughing as he rubbed his head.

His lack of hair is one of the few signs of age Stillwell shows. As he rocks in a recliner in the couple's neat, comfortable home, he looks twenty years younger.

He credits exercise with helping him to stay active.

"I've just been around the block a few times, but I exercise," he said. "I've got routines that I go through nearly every day unless I'm tied up with something else.

"I recommend that everyone ex-

Staff photo by Dean Vincent

Stillwell plays piano in music room of his home.

> 'No, I haven't slowed down yet. I'm still going full-steam. I'll probably slow down when they throw dirt on my face.'

ercise," he added. "It keeps the blood flowing and keeps you going."

One physical activity Stillwell said he enjoys when he has free time is bicycle riding. That gives him the chance to use an object that has been in his life many years.

"I ride a bicycle, the same one I've had for 40 years," he said. "It was a good bike to start with. They don't build them like that any more."

Stillwell keeps pedaling the old bike, even though some advise him to buy a new one.

"Folks get after me about why I haven't gotten another one," Stillwell said. "But it suits me all right."

Another activity he has enjoyed

since his retirement is playing the piano and organ.

He and his wife also stay busy with activities at the church they have attended together since 1937, Second Avenue United Methodist.

Stillwell sings in the church choir and serves as chairman of the church's growth-plus team, which welcomes new church members.

Throughout their long marriage, the Stillwells have kept busy with their family life as well.

The couple has three daughters, nine grandchildren and seven great-grandchildren, Stillwell said.

One daughter, Madeline Dunwoody, lives in Rome. The other two, Suzanne Copeland and Lynn Mashburn, live in Emerson and Cumming, respectively.

Their combined families create quite a crowd in the Stillwell's home during the holidays.

"At Christmas, we have about 30 or 35 around the table," Stillwell said. "We have a nice family, and we have a good time all the time."

Chapter 4

Family

CHILDREN

Children are the pride and joy,
of people everywhere,
They bring us joy and gladness,
their thoughts we always share.

They too are like the sunshine,
as it throws its' beaming light,
For their presence fills a darkened soul,
as moonbeams fill the night.

Children are like the birds above,
as they fly on wings of song,
Sending gladness to all the world,
for they too know no wrong.

Their hearts are pure and sinless,
their eyes blind to sin,
Thoughts so sweet and stainless,
no shame of soul within.

Children are like the flowers sweet,
whose fragrance fills the air,
Their beauty too will ones' heart,
with a love we wish to share.

They are like the trees so tall,
with their arms stretched out above,
Bringing joy throughout the year,
to countless things we love.

Children are like the snowflakes,
as they flutter down from the sky.
For both are pure and spotless,
in the sight of God on high.

Children are a gift from God,
through us He gives them birth,
He sends them to this world of ours,
to spread joy over all the earth.

CHILDREN

Children are the pride and joy, of people everywhere,
they bring us joy and gladness, their thoughts we always share.

They too are like the sunshine, as it throws its beaming light,
for their presence fills a darkened soul, as moonbeams fill the night.

Children are like the birds above, as they fly on winds of song,
sending gladness to all the world, for they too know no wrong.

Their hearts are pure and sinless, their eyes blind to sin,
Thoughts so sweet and stainless, no shame of soul within.

Children are like the flowers sweet, whose fragrance fills the air,
their beauty too will ones' heart, with a love we which to share.

They are like the trees so tall, with their arms stretched out above,
bringing joy throughout the year, to countless things we love.

Children are like snowflakes, as they flutter down from the sky,
for both are pure and spotless, in the sight of God on high.

Children are a gift from God, through us he gives them birth,
he sends them to this world of ours, to spread joy over all the earth.

MY LITTLE GIRLS

My little girls, my precious pearls, sent to me from Him on high,
my little girls with pretty curls, to bring me joy until I die.

You are the sunshine of my heart, the light of every day,
to my life, a precious part, whether close to me or far away.

My little girls with smiling eyes, with radiant cheeks, and a heart so wise,
so full of mischief, but kindly too, you'll always be mine, my whole life through.

You are the joy that fills my life, each morning, noon, and night,
you chase away all strife, and bring me pure delight.

My little girls, my precious pearls, sent to me from up above,
from this day on, 'til life is gone, you'll always be 'til eternity—
My little girls

To Madeline, Suzanne & Battey Lynn

OUR FIRST CHILD

The stork few low one evening, to deliver a bundle of love,
to a boy and girl who were waiting, for a present from above.

Their waiting was soon rewarded, in the late evening sun,
as the stork delivered the bundle, a new life was begun.

It turned out to be a baby girl, though we were hoping for a boy,
but she looked so sweet and beautiful, our disappointment turned
into joy.

The coming months went swiftly by, our child grew more each day,
and soon was crawling about the floor, some words she learned to
say.

A whole year soon had passed us by, each day brought joy and love,
because this child was sent to us, by the angels up above.

We watched her grow down through the years, her beauty, our
pride and joy,
her laughing eyes that childish smile, so glad she's not a boy.

Now she has grown much older, to school, she had to start,
to learn to write her ABCs, of course, she is very smart.

Now here am I so far away, across the deep blue sea,
doing my part to win a fight, so she may always be free.

I think of her all through the day, I pray for her each night,
that God will protect her always, and keep her in his sight.

Now Madeline that ends this story, that I've written just for you,
Daddy wishes you joy and happiness, and success your whole life
through.

Written for Madeline by her Daddy
June 6, 1945 in Manilla, P.I.

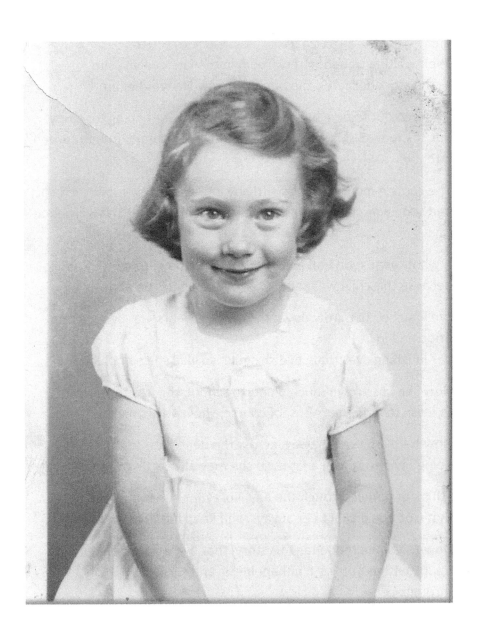

BROWN EYES

One lovely night in June, while the moon was riding high,
A baby girl was sent to me, from somewhere in the sky.

She was a beautiful baby, as anyone could see,
though not because of the very fact, that in some ways she looked like me.

From the very first time I saw her, through the glass where they made me stand,
I knew I would love her always, this child whom we called Suzanne.

Her baby ways were lovable, her smile bright as the skies,
her thoughts so pure and innocent, those lovely big brown eyes.

To me, she looked just like a doll, as she rested in quiet sleep,
and I gave my thanks to Him on high, because he gave me her to keep.

As the months and years went swiftly by, her beauty grew more each day,
I watched her laugh, I saw her cry, I noticed each thing she would say.

Sometimes I gave her a spanking when she told me childish lies,
but it always hurt me more than she, as the tears would fill her eyes.

She gave me countless hours, of pleasure so divine,
and probably a few of worry, when she refused to mind.

But now I'm looking forward, to that great and happy day,
when this cruel war is over, and I go home to stay.

To live there with my loved ones, just as in days gone by,
to play with Sue and the others, while the sun shines in the sky.

Suzanne this ends my poem, only one more thing I wish to say,
may God be with you always, bringing happiness and joy each day.

Written for Suzanne by her daddy
June 6, 1945 in the Phillippines

CURLEY TOP

One year soon after Christmas, a gift was sent to me,
a baby girl with big brown eyes, our third child she would be.

She made us very happy, we knew from the very start,
that she, just like the others, would soon have a place in our hearts.

It gave me much pleasure in the evening, to hold her close to my breast,
and to sing to her songs for children, as she lay there to rest.

I washed her diapers, changed her clothes, would feed her every day,
would take her out to walk with me or often watch her play.

Soon she learned to crawl around, even learned to talk,
started getting into everything, as soon as she could walk.

The way she laughed, the way she smiled, that curly head of hair,
the way she turned that pretty head, the way that she could stare.

Those dancing eyes bright as the stars, that shine so high above,
the way she cuddled in my arms, like a little turtle dove.

Her little arms about my neck, her kiss so pure and sweet,
made my heart so full of joy, my happiness so complete.

My memories of this and other things will carry me through this strife,
my only thoughts through every day, to return to a normal life.

I'll end this ditty by saying, to my daughter Battey Lynn,
you are sweet, so kind and beautiful, so pure so free of sin.

I wish you health and happiness, and all the success in the world,
may your days be filled with contentment, good luck to my curly-headed little girl.

Written for Battey Lynn by her daddy
June 6, 1945, in the Phillippines

<u>TO DADDY – A TOAST</u>

HERE'S TO THE MAN FROM ROME,
WHOM WE CELEBRATE TODAY IN HIS HOME.

WITH HIS WIFE AND THREE LOVELY GIRLS,
WHAT ELSE COULD YOU WANT IN YOUR WORLD?

WHY THREE HANDSOME SONS–IN-LAW AND A PASSLE
OF GREAT AND GRANDKIDS,
WHO'VE SHARED HIS LIFE WITH NO SECRETS HID.

SO HERE WE ARE, A BIRTHDAY TODAY,
I CAN'T BELIEVE IT; 90, YOU SAY!

LET'S DRINK A TOAST TO THE MIRACLE OF LIFE,
AND GOOD GENES, OF COURSE, WITH NO MORE STRIFE.

TO THE MAN WHO BORE US AND GAVE US SUCH LOVE,
GOD BLESS YOU AND KEEP YOU FROM HEAVEN ABOVE!

YOUR THREE GIRLS

November 27, 2007

NO OTHER LIKE MOTHER

There will never be another, like your dear old mother, until life on earth is through,
you'll never find a soul so kind, so faithful, so loyal, and true.

There'll never be one who'll give up their fun, like your mother the whole day long,
do all the work, never try to shirt, and carry on her lips a song.

Throughout this earth, God never gave birth, to one so willing to bear,
your heartaches, or pain, never to complain, your troubles she'll always share.

Besides your mother there is no other, who finds in you no wrong,
she's always there, so fine, so fair, to her you'll always belong.

From baby to man she'll understand, all your needs, your desires, or fears,
it's always her style to carry a smile, bring you cheer throughout the years.

Though her hair turns grey, she is always gay, forever by your side,
with kindly eyes, a heart so wise and a soul overflowing with pride.

There will never be another like your dear old mother, you could search throughout this earth,
from beginning to end she's a boy's best friend because she gave you birth.

I'm sure there's a place where God will embrace, each mother for eternity,
but we'll continue to hold a treasure untold, for in our hearts she will always be.

DEAR SIS

My dearest sis I'm writing this, just dropping you a line,
I hope that all is going well and that you're feeling fine.

I receive your letter most every week, telling me all the news,
this helps my morale to reach the peak, and chase away the blues.

Things are about the same over here, we don't have much to do,
now and then a case of beer, which lasts only a day or two.

It's very hot, plenty of rain, the mosquitoes are bad at night,
still, I have no reason to complain, to gripe just wouldn't be right.

When I think of the price that some have paid, the deeds of
greatness done,
all the sacrifices which were made, before the war was won.

I feel so humble, so contrite, for the debt can never be paid,
to those who really won the fight, that our freedom would never
fade.

I'm thankful that luck was with me, unhurt by shot or shell,
and soon I'm coming home to see, you all whom I love so well.

You've helped me so much these many years, have always been so
kind,
once gave me a home even washed my ears, but never seemed to
mind.

So thanks a mission for everything, there isn't much else to say,
so here's hoping the future will only bring happiness to you each
day.

Give my regards to everyone, tell them to write to me,
here's wishing too, I see you soon, my love always,

C.B.

THE PEST

Many, many, long years ago, when I was young and gay,
I would go to see the girl I loved, the one I still love today.

It seemed to be a family custom, that I couldn't stay very late,
about ten pm she made me leave, so this I found was my fate.

I couldn't get a goodnight kiss, because I soon became aware,
the pest, my girl's dear baby sister, was hidden near the foot of the stair.

So we would walk out to the porch, still wishing for a hug or kiss,
and in the window, pepping out, watched the pest to spoil our bliss.

This thing went on for many weeks, each time I came to call,
I either put up with sister dear, or else she made a haul.

I brought her candy and picture books, a rabbit on Easter too,
but still, she watched when I left, to see what I would do.

So I had to marry this girl of mine, to keep the pest away,
but things have changed since long ago, this is what happens today.

The pest is now grown and beautiful, her dates each night are there,
but it's my kids now, who paying her back, for the times she drove me to despair.

For now, it's my kids that watches whenever her boyfriends come by,
they stand around, get in the way, or see what she might try.

I hope that she by now has learned, just how I used to feel,
when she would watch my every move, so nothing I could conceal.

Probably she will soon marry, so as to get a rest,
or maybe for the same reason as I, to get rid of the pest.

Written to the "Pest" – Beverly

MY MOTHER-IN-LAW #1

When I married some years ago, the deal I got was raw,
besides my wife to keep for life, I got a mother-in-law.

She tells my wife the things I do, nothing to her is right,
I take one drink, she looks around and says, now don't get tight.

I cannot have a minutes peace because she's always there,
telling me what not to do or the things I should wear.

I pick up the phone to talk a bit, she's always on the wire,
telling a neighbor she has a pain, or making me out a liar.

My wife and I get ready to go to a movie or dance nearby,
between us sits my mother-in-law, to leave her home is needless to
try.

My mother-in-law will cuss me out, talk behind my back,
everything I plan to do, about it she makes a crack.

Now I could get along I'm sure, without this ma in law of mine,
without her face around my place, this world would be divine.

But no this luck won't come to me, where I am, she will always be,
she'll follow me to spoil my fun, throughout eternity.

MY MOTHER-IN-LAW #2

We all hear stories of mother in laws, the things they say and do,
their awful tempers, their nagging ways, so heartless through and
through.

They are the butt of countless jokes and probably some are true,
even in songs, they do nothing but wrongs, so this will be news to
you.

My mother-in-law is young and gay, full of fun and sprits too,
and quite pretty, so I would say theses things I swear are true.

My mother-in-law is thoughtful, she even helped me to get a start,
she's kind and very considerate in her is a golden heart.

She has helped me many times, since her daughter I carried away,
and countless times has given us things, without a cent of pay.

She never interferes in my business, stays always in her place,
but is willing to help most any time, and does with a smiling face.

She keeps the kids 'til late at night, when we take in a show,
always willing to lend a hand, if we have some place to go.

Now she is one in a million, to me she's really a pearl,
I even love my mother-in-law, 'cause she's the best one in the
world.

Chapter 5

Daily Thoughts

THANKS

To all of you back there at home,
we want to send our thanks,
for sending us fellows over here,
the ships, the planes, the tanks.

The bullets too must come from you,
the tractor, trucks, and trains,
the peeps, the jeeps, shells and bombs,
and medicine to ease our pains.

The longrange guns, rations by the tons,
our equipment, the clothes we wear,
so thanks to you, for fighting too,
a battle of production there.

The food we eat, the dressings neat,
our tents or metal huts,
the helmets thick, that bullets just kick,
or the stuff to dress our cuts.

You've worked so hard, done good indeed,
and you've helped save many lives,
by getting to us the things we need,
like pistols, gasmasks, and knives.

it's your spirit too, which will carry us through,
to the victory that lies ahead,
we'll keep the planes humming, if you'll keep them comin
and give us plenty of lead.

So accept our thanks from all the ranks,
from privates and generals too,
don't start shirking, just continue working,
and we'll win this war for you.

THANKS

To all of you back there at home, we want to send our thanks,
for sending us fellows over here, the ships, the planes, the tanks.

The bullets too must come from you, the tractor, trucks, and trains,
the people, the jeeps, shells and bombs, and medicine to ease our
pains.

The long-range guns, rations by the tons, our equipment, the
clothes we wear,
so thanks to you, for fighting too, a battle of production there.

The food we eat, the dressings neat, our tents or metal huts,
the helmets thick, that bullets just kick. Or the stuff to dress our
cuts.

You've worked so hard, done well indeed, and you've helped save
so many lives,
by getting to us the things we need, like pistols, gasmask, and
knives.

It's your spirit too, which will carry us through, to the victory that
lies ahead,
we'll keep the planes humming if you'll keep them coming and give
us plenty of lead.

So accept our thanks from all the ranks, from privates and generals
too,
don't start shirking, just continue working, and we'll win this war for
you.

THE MEANING OF A FRIEND

As we travel down this road of life, from beginning to the end,
the thought comes up from time to time, the meaning of a friend.

And as you talk to various ones, their versions are far apart,
a bosom buddy, a pal in need, or someone that helped you start.

Perhaps it's the lady who lives next door or the fellow down the
street,
or the chap on the bus, who was willing to stand, so that you would
have a seat.

A friend could be a clasping hand, a word in time of sorrow,
that tells of love, of prayer, of faith, and helps you reach tomorrow.

Someone has said that a real true friend, is the one who knows you
well,
the good, the bad, the false, the truth will never, never, tell.

Yes, a friend is quite a lot of things, a smile, a tear, a sigh,
a laugh, a frown, a joke or a hug, or maybe a little white lie.

But regardless of where you're rich or poor, wear rags or dress in
style,
the friend for you is h the person who can always make you smile.

It's the one who speaks the kindest word when by chance you've
done some wrong,
who seems to bring out, your very best, who leaves you with a
song.

A friend is one that stands by you, who helps you recognize,
the beauty, the love, the power, the grace, of the Father in the
skies.

I a feeble way I'm trying to say, how much we miss you all,
the fellowship, the food, the fun we had when by your house we'd
call.

Your presence at church, the helping hand, when there were things
to do,
the joke, the smile, the kindly word, when things looked sort of
blue.

So now you see, you've left a space, which no one can refill,
and a lot of folks, in good ole Rome, swear, no one ever will.

Now I'll bring to a close, this poem of verse which I have written
just for you,
and end our love, our prayer, our desire that lives be full and true.

And since we've known you, through these years, we love you like
our kin,
and we'll never forget, this family of Jones the "Real meaning of a
Friend".

IT'S MORNING AGAIN

When the darkness begins to fade, and the morning light breaks through,
the roosters start their crowing and the ground is covered with dew.

The stars above cease to shine, the moon sinks away,
the wind whips up a morning breeze to start the coming day

The birds sing from the treetops or feed their young in the nest,
the cows start mooing from the barnyard, ready to give their best.

The flowers are fresh and fragrant, beautiful for the eyes to see,
the grass too is greener still under the sky or budding tree.

When your clock goes off with a loud bang, you know the night is through,
you must get up to start the day with plenty of things to do.

You find your body rested, your mind fresh and gay,
then the sun again starts coming up to start another day.

The whole world seems refreshed when the morning light breaks through,
the black of night is changed around and the sky is again blue.

So after the night is over and a new day takes a start,
it's morning again throughout the world, so start it with a cheerful heart.

EVENING

When the golden sun seeks in the west, and the birds start winging to their nest.
the sky overhead starts turning gray, and it comes to the end of another day.
>   It's Evening

When the breezes still and the shadows fall, chickens chirp and crickets call,
old man moon stats showing his face, as there in the heavens he takes his place.
>   It's Evening

When twilight falls and all is still, around the barn or by the mill,
the farmers come in from their fields to home the cattle and horses cease to roam.
>   It's Evening

When the grass and flowers are covered with dew and the stars in the skies come peeping through, children come in from their play outside, tired and dirty, but full of pride.
>   It's Evening

When ripples on a stream cast a silvery light, the sinking sun no longer in sight,
when people come home, their work ceased, to find their heaven of rest and peace.
>   It's Evening

When God in heaven up above, looks below on the world he loves, and sees his moon, his stars, and skies, his people at peace before his eyes.
>   It's Evening

THE MORNING AFTER THE NIGHT BEFORE

When I awoke this morning my memory wasn't clear,
I vaguely remember the night before and feel so awful queer.

I pushed down the covers and stumbled out of bed,
my throat was dry, my face was pale, had swimming in my head.

I groped my way to the bathroom, to be sure, I made it quick,
my stomach was going up and down, gosh but I was sick.

After I finished urking, I felt so terribly weak,
but, I knew just what I needed, as for a bottle I started to seek.

I found it in the pantry at once I took a sip,
it quieted my nerves, eased the pain, so I took another nip.

My eyes were red, my lips were white. My muscles felt very sore,
my knees were shaking at every step. So I took a little bit more.

I put on my pants, combed my hair, washed my face, and got in my
shoes,
I stepped up to the window, but still had the morning blues.

My head felt awful dizzy, the shakes I couldn't hide,
during all the day I couldn't eat, eight times I darn near died.

The water I drank was even sweet and it seemed to kindle the fire,
I swore that if I lived through this, never again would I have the
desire.

I tell you I have learned my lesson, this will happen to me no more,
I couldn't stand another time, the morning after the night before.

THE WONDERS OF NATURE

When God made the earth and all within, he thought of everything,
to make the happiness all complete, the things that joy would bring.

He gave us the birds to sing in the trees, with a melody all their
own,
their voices floating through the breeze, with a beauty that to all is
known.

His flowers to are everywhere, in the woods, the valleys, and hills,
their fragrance always fills the air, their beauty always brings a thrill.

In the heavens at night, we have the moon, riding there high in the
skies,
while under it lovers croon, as its loveliness catches their eyes.

We also see the shining stars, watching us from up above,
they seem so near yet very far, with a brightness we've learned to
love.

Then God's rain comes falling down, bring life to all below,
his birds, his people, the seeds in the ground, it makes his rivers
flow.

The golden rays of a setting sun, when at last the day is through,
gives a picture to all until night has begun, makes light for daytime
too.

Most of all will agree the loveliest sight, which will ever meet our
eyes,
is a blanket of snow as it wings its flight or its beauty as on the
world it lies.

God gave us different trees, with colored leaves so gay,
to give shelter to the birds and bees, or build places for us to stay.

Dear God, we thank thee for these things, all the beauties you have sent to earth,
we thank thee for the joy it brings, we thank thee for giving us birth.

SPRING

When the dark days of winter are over, the snow is no longer i
found,
when birds come back from their winter home, Then spring is all
around.

The budding trees by the roadside, A brook where fishes play,
flowers scattered here and there, For winter has gone away.

The air is so refreshing, as the breezes pass you by,
they seem to whisper spring is here, a gift from God on high.

The trees are full of colored leaves, With vines that to them cling,
flowers burst forth with blossoms gay, The birds commence to sing.

The countryside in all its splendor, Gardens planted everywhere,
fruit trees full of blossoms sweet Spring is in the air.

Birds fly around in colors bright, their voices full of song,
bringing joy to all the world in a land where they belong.

We see children playing with faces filled with smiles so bright and
gay,
their joyous laughter fills our hearts, for spring is here to stay.

Spring is full of joyous days, Its fragrance fills the air,
its birds, its trees, its blossoms gay the things that all men share.

I think spring is the very best of the seasons throughout the year,
for it brings us beauty from God above, his gift of beauty and cheer.

THE WIND

No one knows from where it comes, and it cannot be seen,
but you can feel its breath upon your face, so refreshing, and so
clean.

You can hear it blowing through the trees, see the leaves come
falling down,
yet to you, it's only a breeze, blowing things around.

What good does it do for mankind, perhaps someone has said,
it scatters my leaves brings trash around, blows the hats right off
my head.

Well, it brings the water from the ground, with windmills hers and
there,
makes power too for the lights we use, gives fragrance to the air.

It helps some boats and ships to sail and brings to us spring
showers,
without it, Columbus would not have found, this beautiful land of
ours.

Yes, the wind of course has a job to do, right here on God's great
earth,
like the moon, rain, the sun, and you, all the things that he gave
birth.

So when you feel upon your face, the breezes you cannot see,
or see the leaves come falling down, out of a mighty tree.

Or see the sails of some great ship, full of unseen power,
it sent to earth by Him above, who gives us blessings each hour.

Chapter 6

Poems Written for Buddies

I LEFT MY HEART IN NEW ORLEANS

I left my heart in New Orleans,
with a wonderful girl back there,
though I had known her for only a few short weeks,
I knew I would always care.

I remember so clearly the night we met,
on Canal Street there in town,
you were so beautiful as you smiled at me,
on that corner where you I found.

That night we two went dancing,
to a place not far away,
as we sat at the table I looked at you,
you were so sweet and gay.

The next three weeks went swiftly by,
I saw you most every night,
we went to the shows and dances,
or made love under a moon so bright.

One night while standing on your poarch,
you promised always to be true,
to write to me and send your love,
until I came back to you.

Then the time soon came around,
when we would have to part,
For I was going overseas,
leaving with an empty heart.

That very day we had made our plans,
to go to the beach near by,
to play in the sand, watch the tide,
and wish on the stars in the sky.

Now many months have passed us by,
we are thousands of miles apart,
but soon I hope to be back with you,
because you still have my heart.

Written for George Bulrice for his girl he is
going to marry.

89

I LEFT MY HEART IN NEW ORLEANS

I left my heart in New Orleans, with a wonderful girl back there,
though I had known her for only a few short weeks, I knew I would
always care.

I remember so clearly the night we met, on Canal Street there in
town,
you were so beautiful as you smiled at me, on that corner where
you I found.

That night we two went dancing, to a place not far away,
as we sat at the table I looked at you, you were so sweet and gay.

The next three weeks went swiftly by, I saw you almost every night,
we went to the shows and dances or made love under a moon so
bright.

One night while standing on your porch, you promised always to be
true,
to write to me and send your love, until I came back to you.

Then the time soon came around, when we would have to part,
for I was going overseas, leaving with an empty heart.

That very day had made our plans, to go to the beach nearby,
to play in the sand, watch the tide, and wish on the stars in the sky.

Now many months have passed us by, we are thousands of miles
apart,
but soon I hope to be back with you because you still have my
heart.

Written for George Bulrice for his girl he is going to marry.

DO YOU REMEMBER

Do you remember dearest, a few short months ago?
When we were having fun together, in sunshine, moonlight, and
snow.

I remember so well our first meeting, you were walking down the
beach,
through binoculars, I saw you approaching, looking more beautiful
than a Georgia peach.

I'm sure your first impression, of me, was bad I know,
for looking at the girls through glasses is a trick that is pretty low.

But soon we were the best of friends, always on the go,
eating lunch in sidewalk cafes, or attending some Brooklyn show,

I wonder if you still remember, the nights we rode in cars,
or parked in some secluded spot, to watch the moon and stars.

The many times we went swimming, Jones Beach was a favorite
spot,
or perhaps to Leota's East Point House, eating seafood or having a
shot.

The times we had on the boardwalk, watching fireworks color the
sky.
or sitting inside an easy chair, letting the world go by.

I remember very well dear, your smile your winning charm,
those laughing eyes the way you talked, when I held you in my
arms.

I remember too the thrill it was, to have you by my side,
there on the beach with the moon above, as we watched the
ocean's tide.

Do you remember Muriel dear? Those things we used to do,
each day was filled with pleasure, when I was there with you.

Perhaps it won't be very long, until Brooklyn I'll see once more,
then you'll find me just as before, knocking on your door.

Once again we'll go our riding, or swim beneath the stars,
maybe watch the fireworks up above, or drink in the corner bars.

Now I am looking forward dear, and I hope that you are too.
To the day we finish over here, so again I can be with you.

Written for George Shevlin for his girl in Brooklyn, New York.

A REMINDER OF LOVE

Darling, I am sending this your way, as a reminder of my love for you,
I remember well the days gone by, and the things we used to do.

I saw you for the first time, at the Bluebird Cafe in town,
I came in for a bite to eat, and instead there you I found.

It hasn't been so long ago, since you promised to be mine,
and gave to me your very all, making my life so divine.

This is just a short reminder, to tell you I will always be true,
no matter where I have to go, or what I have to do.

I will never forget your winning smile, your laugh, and those big brown eyes,
the reddish glow of your lovely hair, that sparkled like the skies.

The times we would go dancing, to Vets and other places too,
drinking gin spirits, hearing favorite songs, it was heaven to be with you.

This is just a little reminder, of the home I have planned for you,
perhaps some children along the way. When my job over here is through.

Sweetheart your letters mean so much to me, I look forward to them each day,
to read the news from there at home and the other sweet things you say.

Darling this is a short reminder, that soon there will be a day,
when again we'll walk through Fricks Park, and watch the squirrels play.

And again we'll go out dancing, I can hold you in my arms,

look down into your smiling face, and see a thousand charms.

I miss you, dearest, every hour since I had to go away,
my love for you grows more and more, every passing day.

In closing, I might add one thing, I know you'll always be true,
and that you'll be there waiting when I come back to you.

Written for George Wieser for his wife from Braddock,
Pennsylvania.

THOUGHTS OF YOU

It's thoughts of you, my dearest one, that makes my life
worthwhile,
the things we used to say and do, your laugh, your lovely smile.

It brings back many memories when I think of how we met,
in a room behind the drug store, where we would go and set (sit).

You looked so very beautiful, in your uniform of white,
and lovelier still in an evening gown, when we would go out at
night.

You made my life a pleasure, throughout these many years,
through good and bad you've stuck with me, to share my joys,
griefs, or fears.

It's thoughts of our lovely children, the ones you gave to me,
that makes me love you more and more, it's with you I want to be.

You gave me Nipper, big and strong, and later Sheridan Ann,
to bring more joy into our lives, their future we could plan.

It's thoughts of your smiling Irish eyes, that make me dream of you,
your beautiful hair and charming ways, the things you used to do.

May the day come very soon, when together again we'll be,
playing golf, or swimming at Santa Cruz, or at home, at Astoria by
the sea.

Until my job is finished here, I'll continue thinking f you,
making plans for our future years, when I'm home and the war is
through.

Written for Lt. Chapman, for his wife in Santa Cruz, California.

Chapter 7

The City of Rome, GA

HOME IS WHERE THE HEART IS

Is home the place you hang your hat
when the days work is through,
Or a place to go and be alone
when there's nothing you wish to do.

Perhaps it's a place to go and rest
when you're tired and need a bed,
Or the place you always turn too
when you have an aching head.

Could home be a canvas tent
where holes let in the sky,
Or must it be a mansion large
upon a hill so high.

Home could be a crumbling hut
or a house old and grey,
Even a cave in the hillside
is where some wish to stay.

It could be on the oceans
in the desert where life is free,
Or even in some lighthouse
beside the rolling sea.

The Gypsies home where could it be
when they travel by night and day,
Always moving onward
no place they choose to stay.

I think home is in the heart
and ones' heart can be anywhere,
In a cave, a tent, or tumbled down shack,
or out in the open air.

I say home is any place
whether a hut or mansion by the sea,
For home is where your heart is
the place you want to be.

HOME IS WHERE THE HEART IS

Is home the place you hang your hat when the day's work is
through?
Or a place to go and be alone, when there's nothing you wish to do.

Perhaps it's a place to go and rest when you're tired and need a
bed,
or the place you always turn to when you have an aching head.

Could a home be a canvas tent where holes let in the sky?
Or must it be a mansion large upon a hill so high?

Home could be a crumbling hut or a house old and gray,
even a cave in a hillside is where some wish to stay.

It could be on the oceans, in the desert where life is free,
or even in some lighthouse beside the rolling sea.

The Gypsy's home where could it be when they travel by night and
day,
always moving onward, no place they choose to stay.

I think home is in the heart, and one's heart can be anywhere,
in a cave, a tent, or tumbled down shack, or out in the open air.

I say home is any place, whether a hut or mansion by the sea,
for home is where your heart is, the place you want to be.

WHAT IS ROME

What is Rome bt a city small, beneath some seven hills?
Or a friendly town deep in the south, where travelers find many
thrills.

Home is more than a city small. Wher hills point to the sky,
or where farmers bring their goods to sell, Rome is more than
meets the eye.

Rome is its homes, whether old or new, whether a shack or a
mansion fine,
where its children grow up through the years, to be leaders,
whether yours or mine.

Rome is the clock there on the hill, where we tell the time of day,
Rome is the streets, the corner lots, where countless children play.

Rome is its churches with steeples high, where the Saviour is
brought to all,
no matter what color or what creed, its churches will never fail.

Rome is its schools where children learn, the difference between
right and wrong,
from A B C's to the highest degrees, in language, music, or song.

Then Rome is the hospitals large and clean, where the doctors your
case will explain,
a place where any and all may go, when in sickness or in pain.

Rome is its plants and factories large, where clothes and stoves are
made,
and countless things used by us all. Rome's business will never fade.

Yes, Rome is the shopping center, where people from miles around,
come into town most every day, to see what can be found.

I believe I've answered the question, if not, I sure have tried,
to explain to you what Rome is, in a short, Rome is people and a city
full of pride.

THE HILLS OF ROME

Some folks dream of mountains, others the deep blue sea,
and then there's those who choose the west where they would like
to be.

Some men like the prairie, others like the coast,
some even say the desert sand is the place they like most.

Now I prefer a city small, with lots of growing trees,
with gardens here, flowers there budding in the breeze.

Where I can walk down any street and surely meet a friend,
or step next door to a neighbor for sugar she is willing to lend.

Or ride down any main street in a car old in style,
and see the sights which are very few, but always bring a smile.

The hills of home is the place I choose as the one I like the best,
where I can walk down many hills or lie in the shade and rest.

Now this place of which I'm speaking has several rivers wide,
more beautiful than the oceans with their fall and rising tide.

There are seven hills around my town, each pointing to the sky,
each one a scene of beauty, when you gaze out from on high.

One hill is a resting place, where many great souls lie,
because they choose the hills of home when their time comes to
die.

Then you'll find a college, where girls their lessons learn,
from here you can see the beauty of each valley and river turn.

Then other hills bring memories of many dark days gone by,
where our men of gray died for a cause, and now under crosses lie.

Now I could keep on writing about the hills of home.
about each spot of beauty, the places I would roam.

Or about my wife and children, whose waiting for me there,
and of the things, we'll plan and do, when again their joys I'll share.
So as to end this story, about the town called Rome,
I'll simply say it can't be beat, for a place to make a home.

No matter where I wander, no matter where I roam,
I'll always return to the spot I love, the beautiful hills of home.

THE CITY CLOCK

Standing on a hill so high, with hands that point above,
you'll find the face of the city clock, near a spot we dearly love.

She stands there in all her glory, against the pale blue sky,
while under her a city grows, in the distance meadows, lie.

The city clock is something more than just to give the time,
or a thing for little guys like me to a poem of it to rhyme.

She stands there like a lighthouse, that guides lost ships at sea,
or as a symbol of the many things, that made our country free.

At night she is a guiding light, for travelers near and far,
to follow the rays of her shining face, as the wise men followed a
star.

This old clock has stood there almost from the city's start,
a thing of beauty to Romans, the beat of a cities heart.

It sees the joys and sorrows, of all for miles around,
as her face looks down the hillside or through the streets of town.

How this old clock will stand there, perhaps for centuries long,
with her face looking up as if to God, in prayers of heavenly song.

The Stillwell family reunion on August 9, 2014

C.B. had 3 daughters, 9 grandchildren, 13 great-grandchildren, and 1 great-great-grandchild. At the time of his passing, there were 5 generations alive in the family.

Isaiah 59:21 KJV The Blessing

"As for me, this *is* my covenant with them, saith the LORD; My spirit that *is* upon thee, and my words which I have put in thy mouth, shall not depart out of thy mouth, nor out of the mouth of thy seed, nor out of the mouth of thy seed's seed, saith the LORD, from henceforth and forever."

Made in the USA
Monee, IL
27 August 2021